THE Saint Nick STORY

Written by Kate Davis

Illustrated by Jared Tohlen

Sneaking in quietly, a stranger at night,
Normally thoughts that would give us a fright!

But not around Christmas, we've heard how it goes,
St. Nick fills stockings, with presents and bows!

The stories are fun, and the gifts are too,
But why do we celebrate the way that we do?

We know Christmas Day
is clearly about
The birth of our Savior,
as the angels did shout!

So tell me old friend,
I am listening still,
How did St. Nick
become such a thrill?

Well I'm here to tell you
a story of love
About the Jolly Old Man
and his "gifts from above."

Saint Nick was a man,
who cared a great deal
For kids who had lives
full of heartache and fear.

One night, three sisters sat
   scared on their cot,
Sleepless and afraid of what
   morning light brought.

They hadn't enough
   to survive in their home,
So they were to be sold as slaves,
   separated and alone.

Well, Nicholas heard
    of this terrible fate,
And rushed to their aid,
    not a moment too late!

As their stockings hung drying
    by the fire that eve,
In flew a gift
    their eyes could not believe!

Through their opened window,
    he tossed coins made of gold.
St. Nick bought their freedom
    from out in the cold.

The story is told that
    as the girls watched with glee,
Money fell in their stockings,
    1, 2, and 3!

We may never know
just how many names
Would make up the list
of those Santa spared pain.

But what we do know,
and it's with a big cheer:
We can try to be like Nicholas
come Christmas each year!

We can care more about
our neighbors in need,
Than what it might cost
to let go of our greed.

When we choose to give
so that others receive
The Christmas Story continues
through those who believe!

So put aside your list
    of naughty and nice,
And extend a gift of love,
    no matter the price.

I imagine St. Nick
    would be happier still,
If we celebrated his legacy
    by daily doing God's will!

A Note from the Author,

Each year of child-rearing seems to pass more quickly than the last, and I am increasingly convinced that our time of influence is short. Little kids observe every moment, and we don't get to choose what they remember or emulate. This truth is ever-present in my mind as I navigate the holidays, and consequently our family does not teach the belief in Santa Claus. I hold no judgement for those that do, but personally, I find it too hard to reconcile the message of a naughty and nice list with the undeserved gift of Jesus. I have discovered that you can build a lot of fun memories celebrating Advent that provide the excitement for Christmas we all know and enjoy.

However, kids are both observant and curious, so the bombardment of North Pole themed Christmas festivities draws questions. I wrote this story to bridge the gap. We can all learn a lot about God by observing his work in people like Saint Nicholas.

I hope this book provides for you another opportunity to talk about God's Extravagant Gift with the children you love this Christmas.

Merry Christmas,
Kate

Below are a few ideas on how to include The Saint Nick Story in your Christmas celebration:

Celebrate by Giving

December 6th is Saint Nicholas' Day. To celebrate, plan a get-together and put together "stocking" care-packages or gifts to give to someone in need. (For example: nursing home, homeless shelter, children's hospital, etc.) Involve your kids and your neighbors as much as possible in the gathering of supplies and delivering of gifts. Read the book together and have fun!

Restore Meaning to the Stockings Tradition

Consider reading this book before stockings are opened and explain that we have stockings to remind us that God hears the prayers of the broken and often answers those prayers through his people. In addition, choose carefully the items that stuff your stockings. We put a donation gift specific to each person. (For example: One year, a family member donated to an organization that provides jerseys and shoes to underprivileged kids who want to play basketball in honor of my husband, who loves basketball.)

Other Ideas

Stuff stockings with fair-trade chocolate coins (to symbolise the coins St. Nick gave away), gifts that are purchased for a good cause, or a "for others" gift card that they can use to bless someone spontaneously. Consider writing out a prayer for each stocking recipient that focuses on their impact in the world for God's Kingdom. Get creative and let your gifts tell a greater story.

Proceeds from this book will be donated to A21.

A21 is a non-profit organization fuelled by the radical hope–that human beings everywhere will be rescued from bondage and completely restored. By supporting A21, we are joining them as the new abolition-ists of the 21st century. Slavery is often talked about in numbers.

Millions of slaves.
A $150 billion industry.
1% ever rescued.

Those statistics are daunting—and they lose the human element. The heart of A21 is for the one. The one woman, the one man, the one child trapped and exploited, unable to see another end to their story. But A21 sees the one, and fights for the one. We support A21 so that survivors of human trafficking can be given freedom, independence, and the chance at a better story.

"For it is by grace you have been saved, through faith—and this is not from yourselves, it is the gift of God—not by works, so that no one can boast. For we are God's handiwork, created in Christ Jesus to do good works, which God prepared in advance for us to do."

Ephesians 2:8–10